Memories

RAVETTE PUBLISHING

First published in 2014 by
Ravette Publishing Limited
PO Box 876, Horsham
West Sussex RH12 9GH

ISBN: 978-1-84161-384-0

Be strong and of a good Courage.

Onward,
Christian soldiers,
Marching as to war,
With the Cross of Jesus
Going on before.

Christ the Royal Master
Leads against the foe;
Forward into battle,
See, his banners go!

KISS ME GOOD-BYE (1).

"Tommy, boy, it's time that you were leaving;
    Colonel's waiting on the barrack square;
There's the sergeant-major saying things, I'll wager,
    'Cos you are not there."
Said the lassie, to her soldier sweetheart,
    "Soon you'll march in line,
But ere I part from you, come a bit closer, do;
    Place your lips to mine."

KISS ME GOOD-BYE (2).

Kiss me good-bye, my little soldier boy, for when you're gone, you
    know, I'll miss you so.
When you hear that bugle call, Johnny, get your gun and your
    sword and your pistol, marching off you'll go.
Say you'll remember what you promised me ;
    You know you said I'd be your only joy ;
Think of the girl who's missing all your kissing,
    Come back, soon, my little soldier boy.

BAMFORTH (Copyright).

WORDS BY PERMISSION OF THE STAR MUSIC PUBLISHING CO., LONDON.

SANDY, BOY (1).

"Sandy, boy, the pipes are calling, over glen and mountain
  side,
  Duty calls, my soldier lad, buckle on your tartan plaid!"
Said the bonnie Hieland lassie, as they parted by the Dee,
" For, where'er you go, my love, I know you'll leave your
  heart with me."

SANDY, BOY (2).

"Sandy, boy, my soldier laddie, when you're far from Scotland's shore
Dinna forget your ain wee lassie.
Keep the bonnie heather we gathered together.
I hear those pipers playing, and my sad heart beats with joy;
I'll be feelin' awfu' proud, ye ken, to see the Cameron men,
And my ain true Sandy boy."

BANFORTH (Copyright)

I LOVE MY MOTHERLAND (1).

Motherland tho' the mighty seas divide us,
  And your sons were scatter'd one and all,
There came a day—your fam'ly were united,
  'Twas the day they heard your call.
Other nations ask the reason why
From each of us they hear this proud reply.

BAMFORTH COPYRIGHT.   WORDS BY PERMISSION OF THE STAR MUSIC PUBLISHING CO. LONDON.

⸻ I LOVE MY MOTHERLAND (2). ⸺

I love my Motherland, and wherever I may be,
There is no other land like the Motherland to me;
I may be far away, over miles of ocean blue,
But Motherland, dear Motherland, my heart is still with you!

THE TRUMPETER (1).

Trumpeter, what are you sounding now?
   Is it the call I'm seekin'?
"You'll know the call," said the Trumpeter tall,
   "When my trumpet goes a speakin'
I'm rousin' 'em up, I'm wakin' 'em up,
   The tents are astir in the valley,
And there's no more sleep with the sun's first peep,
   For I'm sounding the old Reveille.'
Rise up!" said the Trumpeter tall.

THE TRUMPETER (2).

Trumpeter, what are you sounding now?
Is it the call i'm seekin'?
"Can't mistake the call," said the Trumpeter tall,
"When my trumpet goes a speakin'.
I'm urgin' 'em on, they're scamperin' on,
There's a drummin' of hoofs like thunder,
There's a madd'nin' shout as the sabres flash out,
For I'm soundin' the 'Charge,' no wonder!
And it's Hell!" said the Trumpeter tall.

TAKE ME BACK TO DEAR OLD BLIGHTY (1)

Jack Dunn, son of a gun, over in France to-day,
Keeps fit, doing his bit, up to his eyes in clay;
Each night, after a fight, to pass the time along,
He's got a little gramophone that plays this song.

BAMFORTH COPYRIGHT   WORDS BY PERMISSION OF THE STAR MUSIC PUBLISHING CO., LONDON

TAKE ME BACK TO DEAR OLD BLIGHTY. (2)

Take me back to dear old Blighty, put me on the train
    for London town,
Take me over there, drop me anywhere,
Birmingham, Leeds, or Manchester—well, I don't care !
I should love to see my best girl, cuddling up again we
    soon shall be ;
Whoa ! Tiddley-iddley-ighty, hurry me home to Blighty—
    Blighty is the place for me.

HE ROSES HAVE MADE ME REMEMBER (1).
(ALL THAT I TRIED TO FORGET.)

Roses of June, once more in bloom.
Whisper their message divine;
They seem to say, love lives alway,
Happiness yet may be mine.

THE ROSES HAVE MADE ME REMEMBER (2).
(ALL THAT I TRIED TO FORGET.)

The roses have made me remember all that I tried to forget,
The past with its pain comes back again, filling my heart
   with regret;
In mem'ry I live once again, dear, those sweet, happy days
   when we met:
The roses have made me remember—remember all that I
   tried to forget.

BY ARRANGEMENT WITH MESSRS FRANCIS, DAY & HUNTER, THE PUBLISHERS OF THE MUSIC.

THERE'S A LONG, LONG TRAIL (1).

Nights are growing very lonely, days are very long,
I'm a-growing weary, only list'ning for your song;
Old remembrances are thronging thro' my memory,
Thronging till it seems the world is full of dreams,
Just to call you back to me.

THERE'S A LONG, LONG TRAIL (2).

There's a long, long trail a-winding into the land of my dreams,
Where the nightingales are singing and a white moon beams;
There's a long, long night of waiting, until my dreams all come true,
Till the day when I'll be going down that long, long trail with you.

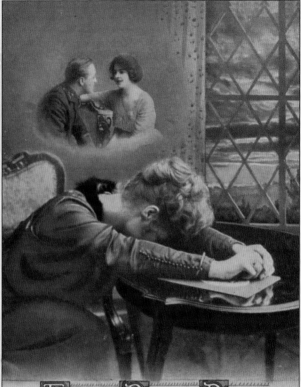

Hearts Bowed Down (1)

THE heart bowed down by weight of woe, to weakest hopes
    will cling,
To thought and impulse, while they flow, that can no comfort bring,
    That can, that can no comfort bring.
With those exciting scenes will blend, o'er pleasure's pathway thrown,
But mem'ry is the only friend that grief can call its own,
That grief can call its own, that grief can call its own.

ᚻEARTS ᛒOWED ᛞOWN (2)

ᚦHE mind will in its worst despair still ponder o'er the past,
On moments of delight that were too beautiful to last,
That were too beautiful to last.
To long departed years extend, its visions with them flown,
For mem'ry is the only friend that grief can call its own,
That grief can call its own, that grief can call its own.

YES, LET ME LIKE A SOLDIER FALL (1).

Yes! let me like a soldier fall, upon some open plain;
This breast expanding for the ball, to blot out ev'ry stain.
Brave manly hearts confer my doom, that gentler ones may tell,
How e'er forgot, unknown my tomb, I like a soldier fell,
How e'er forgot, unknown my tomb, I like a soldier fell,
I like a soldier fell.

BAMFORTH COPYRIGHT.

YES, LET ME LIKE A SOLDIER FALL (2).

I only ask of that proud race, which ends its blaze in me,
To die, the last, and not disgrace its ancient chivalry;
Tho' o'er my clay no banner wave, nor trumpet requiem swell;
Enough they murmur o'er my grave, he like a soldier fell,
Enough they murmur o'er my grave, he like a soldier fell,
He, like a soldier fell.

Ave Maria

Ave Maria, hear my cry,
O guide my path where ⌣
· · · · no harm is nigh;
O turn thy heart to earth and see
My lonely heart, and comfort me!

Words by permission of Ascherberg, Hopwood & Crew, Ltd., London.

Avé Maria

2

MOTHER, SEE MY TEARS ARE FALLING,
THOU HAST ALSO SORROW KNOWN,
LIFE, AH, IT IS SO DREARY,
MY HEART IT IS SO WEARY,
OH, LEAVE ME NOT ALONE!
 MOTHER, HEAR ME IN THE LIGHT,
LOOK DOWN ON ME, MY COMFORT BE,
AND GUIDE MY STEPS ARIGHT!
 MOTHER HEAR ME WHERE THOU ART,
AND GUARD AND GUIDE MY ACHING HEART.

SOMEWHERE A VOICE IS CALLING (1).

Dusk, and the shadows falling
O'er land and sea;
Somewhere a voice is calling,
Calling for me!

SOMEWHERE A VOICE IS CALLING (2)

Night and the stars are gleaming,
  Tender and true,
Dearest! my heart is dreaming,
  Dreaming of you!

HAD I BUT KNOWN (1).

Had I but known that ev'ry word I spoke, dear,
Went to your heart and lingered there—
I would have searched each golden page of love, dear,
And chosen ev'ry word with care.

BY PERMISSION OF THE LAWRENCE WRIGHT MUSIC CO. DENMARK ST. LONDON W.C.

BAMFORTH COPYRIGHT

HAD I BUT KNOWN (2)

Had I but known that ev'ry gift I offered
　　Was naught without my love so true—
I would have given whatsoe'er you craved for—
　　My love—my life—my all to you.

BY PERMISSION OF THE LAWRENCE WRIGHT MUSIC CO., DENMARK ST LONDON, W C.

IN SWEET SEPTEMBER (1).

YOU love me not, or else you would remember
  All that you were, and all you said to me,
Only last year, last year in sweet September,
  Under the stars beside the radiant sea!
You love me not! or else while I am yearning,
  You could not stand with folded hands apart,
With cold, calm eyes, that once with tears were burning,
  Tears of wild love, against my beating heart
Only last year, only last year, only last year in sweet
    September

IN SWEET SEPTEMBER (2).

YOU loved me then—by every tender token
   You loved me then—what profit now to tell?
The chain was sweet, but now the chain is broken,
   And I am nothing, loving you so well!
You loved me then! you love me now no longer!
   Go by, forget, or hate me if you will!
Whate'er it be, I know my love is stronger,
   Thro' all, in all, I only love you still
Only last year! Only last year! Ah, love, my love! do
     you remember?
Only last year! Only last year! Only last year in sweet
     September

UNTIL (1).

No rose in all the world until you came,
   No star until you smiled upon life's sea;
No song in all the world until you spoke,
   No hope until you gave your heart to me.

UNTIL (2).

O rose, bloom ever in my lonely heart,
   O star, shine steadfast with your light divine;
Ring on, O song, your melody of joy,
   Life's crowned at last, and love, is ever mine.

ABSENT (1).

Sometimes, between long shadows on the grass,
The little truant waves of sunshine pass;
My eyes grow dim with tenderness the while,
Thinking I see thee, thinking I see thee smile.

ABSENT (2).

And sometimes, in the twilight gloom apart,
The tall trees whisper, whisper heart to heart;
From my fond lips the eager answers fall,
Thinking I hear thee, thinking I hear thee call.

O DRY THOSE TEARS (1).

O dry those tears, and calm those fears,
 Life is not made for sorrow
'Twill come, alas! but soon 'twill pass,
 Clouds will be sunshine to-morrow.
'Twill come, alas! but soon 'twill pass,
 Clouds will be sunshine to-morrow.

O DRY THOSE TEARS (2)

O lift thine eyes to the blue skies,
  See how the clouds do borrow
Brightness, each one, straight from the sun ;
  So is it ever with sorrow.
'Twill come, alas ! but soon 'twill pass,
  Clouds will be sunshine to-morrow.
Then lift thine eyes to the blue skies,
  Clouds will be sunshine to-morrow.
O dry those tears, life is not made for sorrow.

JUST YOU (1).

What are my thoughts to-night? They're of you!
Where is my heart to-night? Gone with you!
Where is my hope to-night? It's in you!
What is my prayer to-night? 'Tis for you!

JUST YOU (2).

How can I live to-night? Not seeing you!
Why do I weep to-night? 'Cause of you!
Why burn my lips to-night? Kisses for you!
Whom seeks my soul to-night? You, just you!

BAMFORTH (copyright)   By permission of G. Ricordi & Co., 265 Regent St., Lond. W.1

COMING HOME (1).

There is many a step goes lighter, coming home,
There is many an eye grows brighter, coming home;
All the way seems to remind you of sweet memories
that bind you
To dear distant days behind you, coming home!

COMING HOME (2).

You forget your load of sorrow, coming home,
It will wait until the morrow, coming home;
You can see the kind smiles beaming, and the tender
    eyes a-gleaming,
Oh! the longing and the dreaming, coming home!
Ah! Oh, the longing and the dreaming, coming home!

Other Bamforth titles available ...

	ISBN	Price
World War One Series:		
Till We Meet Again	978-1-84161-383-3	£5.99
Saucy Seaside Humour:		
Love Will Find A Way	978-1-84161-367-3	£5.99
Down with Drink	978-1-84161-368-0	£5.99
That's the Way To Do It!	978-1-84161-372-7	£5.99
Not a Care in the World	978-1-84161-373-4	£5.99